SH*T
ROUGH
DRAFTS

SH*T ROUGH DRAFTS

POP CULTURE'S FAVORITE BOOKS, MOVIES, AND TV SHOWS AS THEY MIGHT HAVE BEEN

Paul Laudiero

CHRONICLE BOOKS

SAN FRANCISCO

Library of Congress Cataloging-in-Publication Data

Laudiero, Paul.
  Sh*t rough drafts : pop culture's favorite books, movies, and TV shows as
they might have been / Paul Laudiero.
     pages cm
  ISBN 978-1-4521-3130-6 (pbk.)
  1. Popular culture—Humor. 2. Authorship—Humor. I. Title. II. Title: Shit
rough drafts.

  PN6231.P635L38 2014
  818'.602—dc23

                              2013040352

Manufactured in China

MIX
Paper from
responsible sources
FSC® C008047

Designed by Lydia Ortiz

10 9 8 7 6 5 4 3

Chronicle Books LLC
680 Second Street
San Francisco, California 94107
www.chroniclebooks.com

CONTENTS

INTRODUCTION

When I decided to assemble this collection of terrible rough drafts, people told me it was "impossible," and "stupid," and that I was "three months behind on rent," and that I "really need to pay the rent," or I was going to be "thrown out," and that, "no," I can't "borrow the car." But did I let the haters get me down? No.

Instead I set out in a stolen 2002 Toyota Prius to track down as many drafts as I could. It wasn't easy. Writers are reclusive, secretive creatures, and I was forced to break into homes, museums, libraries, safes, studies, and even crypts (I'm talking about you, Christopher Nolan). I've been arrested hundreds of times, lost an ear (booby traps: thanks a lot, Kafka!), and am currently on the run from the Hemingway estate. I had to fake my own death just to escape J. K. Rowling's assassins. Michael Crichton? He has an *actual* velociraptor guarding his manuscripts. I suffered for these drafts.

Was it worth it? No. Absolutely not. I'm missing three fingers and haven't slept in a warm bed for months. But once you've done the things I've had to do, you don't turn back. I had to show the world that these writers are but mortals like you and me. They toiled and suffered over each line and it wasn't until the pages were bleeding with red ink that they could grow. Before each *New York Times* bestseller climbed the ranks or Academy Award winning film won the Oscar, it was a sh*t rough draft.

So as you turn these pages, don't think about me, on a life raft in the middle of the Pacific, paddling against the trade winds back to my publisher in San Francisco with nothing to eat but a tattered copy of *Robinson Crusoe*. I'll be fine. This is the life I chose. Think about these drafts, these terrible drafts, and the suffering the authors endured to get to the great finished works we know and love. The secret? They just worked hard. They spent hours each day slaving at a desk, in a coffee shop, a bar, or a windowless closet free from distraction, laboring toward perfection.

"The first draft of anything is sh*t," Hemingway once said.

I aim to prove just that.

THE

CLASSICS

"Good Morning Mr. Sense!"
Mr. Sensibility said.
"How did you sleep?"

"Great!" said Mr. Sense,
"Since I am a man and
don't have to worry
about marriage."

They both laughed.

SENSE AND SENSIBILITY
by Jane Austen
(1811)

"She is tolerable, but not black enough to tempt me."

Mr. Darcy was into black women, and there was nothing Elizabeth Bennet could do about it.

Yet.

PRIDE AND PREJUDICE
by Jane Austen
(1813)

Macbeth

All: Double, double, toil + trouble
fire burn and couldron bubble

Second Witch: Fillet a fenny snake
In the couldron boil + bake
eye of newt and a touch
of Cinnamon
A pinch of sugar, now stir
it quick again.

MACBETH
by William Shakespeare
(1606)

Abandon all hope,
ye who enter here —

— DEPRESSING

Welcome to Hell!

↳ TOO HAPPY...

Stop Smiling

Optimists Beware

Leave your shoes   CONFUSING
(and hope) at the door

Abandon all jackets,
because it's gonna be
hot in here

THE DIVINE COMEDY: THE INFERNO
by Dante Alighieri
(1308)

Thou shalt not

TOO PREACHY →

~~Don't~~

PLEASE DO NOT

Be advised

Try to AVOID

~~USE CAUTION~~

(Must) use caution

Be NICE

DON'T BE (ASSHOLES)

I WILL BE SO ~~ANGRY~~ IF

THE BIBLE: "EXODUS"

~~In the beginning~~
~~Once upon a time~~
There was this one night...
I know this ~~crazy~~ story
Hello please read this
~~A long time ago in a~~ ← WHO TALKS LIKE THIS?
I swear this is true
Listen up, dummies
Read the whole thing

THE BIBLE: "GENESIS"

To reign is worth ambition,
though in Hell:

Better to reign in Hell
than to serve ~~drinks~~ in Heaven.

PARADISE LOST
by John Milton
(1667)

Quothe the Raven, "Nevermore."

"Birds can't talk!"
I screamed back.

I let him ~~stay~~ though,
because I was pretty lonely.

"THE RAVEN"
by Edgar Allan Poe
(1845)

The Time Machine

"That reminds me! In changing my jacket
I found...."
The Time traveler paused, put his hand
in his pocket, then pulled it out with
his middle finger in the air.

THE TIME MACHINE
by H. G. Wells
(1895)

War and Peace

~~War + Peace~~

~~Fighting and Loving~~

Arguing and kissing

Battles then smokin' weed

Punching and Sexin

Bloodshed + Hugs

WAR AND PEACE
by Leo Tolstoy
(1869)

Happy families are all alike;

every unhappy family is Russian.

LEO — COME BY AND LETS
HAVE A CUP OF TEA AND TALK...
YOU DOING OK?

ANNA KARENINA
by Leo Tolstoy
(1878)

Dr. Jekyll and Mrs. Hyde

Dr. Jekyll drank the potion and
felt his body start to change.
and change.

and change.

DR. JEKYLL AND MR. HYDE
by Robert Louis Stevenson
(1886)

Jonathan held the garlic up
to Dracula, who screamed
"Aaaahh! I hate that vegetable!"

Jonathan paused for a moment.
"Is garlic a fruit or a vegetable?"
"It doesn't have seeds, right?"
"I don't think so..."
"Yeah, fruits have seeds."
"Really?"
"Yep."
"What about kiwis?"
"Kiwis have seeds."
"Where?"

DRACULA
by Bram Stoker
(1897)

Frankenstein

by Mary Shelley

"What do you do in your room all day?" his landlady asked him. "I smell funny smells and hear strange noises all the time."

"I bake," replied Dr. Frankenstein.

This was true, as he was working on his scone recipe at the time.

Also, he was building a monster.

FRANKENSTEIN
by Mary Shelley
(1818)

"Tom, I didn't know you were an uncle!? What's your nephew's name?"

"Cabin."

UNCLE TOM'S CABIN
by Harriet Beecher Stowe
(1852)

"We're hunting a great white whale called Moby Dick."

"Moby what?"

"Dick"

"Come again?"

"Dick."

"Can you spell it?"

"D - I - c - k"

"You chose this name?"

MOBY DICK
by Herman Melville
(1851)

The Grapes of (Wrath)

The Angry Grapes

(Pissed-Off) Grapes

Raging ~~Raisins~~

~~Grapes~~ with Issues

Graaaapes!!! (in angry voice)

~~The Apples of Wrath~~ HAS TO BE
GRAPES
~~Grapes with Gripes~~

THE GRAPES OF WRATH
by John Steinbeck
(1939)

Tom stood close to Becky.
"Would you like to get married?"
"Not without a pre-nup."

ARENT THEY A LITTLE YOUNG?

THE ADVENTURES OF TOM SAWYER
by Mark Twain
(1876)

"Can I just call you
African-American Jim?"

Huck asked.

THE ADVENTURES OF HUCKLEBERRY FINN
by Mark Twain
(1884)

It was ~~the best of times,~~
~~It was the worst of times.~~

(It was so so)

~~It was~~ an alright time

Some people had it good,
others not so good.

It was comme-ci comme-ça

It was sort of ~~blah~~

Eh (shrugs shoulders) it was okay

A TALE OF TWO CITIES
by Charles Dickens
(1859)

Great Expectations

"My name is Miss Havisham. What is yours?"

"Pip."

"Pit?"

"Pip"

"Pib?"

"Pip."

"Pop."

"No. Pip."

"Who is pop?"

Charles ... its just this for 300 pages ...
We LOVE it.

GREAT EXPECTATIONS
by Charles Dickens
(1860)

Gulliver looked around.
Everyone on this new island
was under six inches high.
"Where am I?" he asked aloud.
"London!" the little people
exclaimed.

GULLIVER'S TRAVELS
by Jonathan Swift
(1726)

Robinson looked at the man he had just saved.

"I'll name you after my favorite day of week: Monday!"

— DANIEL.

THIS IS THE WORST DAY OF THE WEEK.

ROBINSON CRUSOE
by Daniel Defoe
(1719)

The Prince — YOU ARE NOT A PRINCE

by (Prince) Niccolò Machiavelli

Princes are basically just baby kings. In fact, the word "prince" is just Latin for "baby king" — NO IT'S NOT

THE PRINCE
by Niccolò Machiavelli
(1532)

"My name is Athos, and these are my friends Porthos and Aramis. We are the Three Musketeers!"

"I'm D'Artagnan! Can I join?"
"Do you not understand what the word three means?"

30

THE THREE MUSKETEERS
by Alexandre Dumas
(1844)

The Three Musketeers

"I'm Athos, and these are my friends Porthos and Aramis. What's your name?"

"D'Artagnan!"

"What?"

"D'Artagnan."

"Spell it."

"Capitol D, apostrophe, capitol A..."

"Whatever...."

THE THREE MUSKETEERS
by Alexandre Dumas
(1844)

Sherlock Holmes - Speckled Band

"I've solved the case of the Speckled Band, Watson!"

"Oh good, Sherlock."

"Quick question, is it true that your middle name is `Speckled Band`?"

"No sir, it's Harold."
"Nevermind then, Watson. Nevermind."

THE ADVENTURES OF SHERLOCK HOLMES:
"THE ADVENTURE OF THE SPECKLED BAND"
by Sir Arthur Conan Doyle
(1892)

Sherlock Holmes – Red-Headed League

"Watson! I've cracked the case of the red-headed league!"

"Really? Who was it?"

Sherlock took a quick step towards Watson.

"It's –" He knocked Watson's hat to the ground, revealing a head of dark brown hair.

"Nevermind, Watson."

THE ADVENTURES OF SHERLOCK HOLMES:
"THE ADVENTURE OF THE RED-HEADED LEAGUE"
by Sir Arthur Conan Doyle
(1892)

"Watson! I have finally solved the mystery of the hound!"

He slowly raised a finger and pointed it at Watson's face.

"Sherlock, for the tenth time, I'm not a hound. I'm a doctor."

THE HOUND OF THE BASKERVILLES
by Sir Arthur Conan Doyle
(1901)

Jane Eyre

"You keep your insane wife locked up in the attic? Why not a hospital?"
"Too expensive. Now kiss me you fool!"

JANE EYRE
by Charlotte Brontë
(1847)

"What do you mean you don't have a bathroom?"
I asked.

Captain Nemo smiled.
"We just hold it"

TWENTY THOUSAND LEAGUES UNDER THE SEA
by Jules Verne
(1870)

"Bark, bark, woof, bark, woof,"
Buck said as he shook the snow
from his fur.

DOGS
CAN'T
TALK

"Woof, woof, bark, woof, bark,"
Buck peed on a tree.

"Bark Bark bark woof woof
woof."

THE CALL OF THE WILD
by Jack London
(1903)

"I finished the picture of you, Dorian," Basil said. "I hope you like it!"

Dorian stared at the picture for a moment.

"Basil... why am I naked?"

THE PICTURE OF DORIAN GRAY
by Oscar Wilde
(1890)

THE FUN GATSBY
THE NICE GATSBY
THE COOLEST GATSBY ←
THE GABBY GATSBY
THE GATSBY GATSBY ?
THE #1 GATSBY
THE CHUBBY GATSBY
THE LAST GATSBY

THE GREAT GATSBY
by F. Scott Fitzgerald
(1925)

"Why do you keep calling me old sport?"

Gatsby leaned in close and whispered, "Because I can't remember your stupid name."

THE GREAT GATSBY
by F. Scott Fitzgerald
(1925)

"You can't repeat the past."

"Can't repeat the past?" Gatsby cried incredulously. He leaned in close with a crazy look in his eyes. "Guess who just bought a time machine?"

THE GREAT GATSBY
by F. Scott Fitzgerald
(1925)

"Alright Doctor, get rid of them."
Without hesitation, he chopped
both of my arms off with a
machete. It hurt, but I didn't cry,
because I am a man and men don't
cry.

"Farewell arms!" I said.

A FAREWELL TO ARMS
by Ernest Hemingway
(1929)

Santiago was a man, and men fish.
Fishing is the best thing a man
can do. Other than bullfighting.
~~I love bullfighting.~~
ERNEST, EVERYTIME, WHY?

THE OLD MAN AND THE SEA
by Ernest Hemingway
(1952)

The sheep began to bleet:
"Four legs good!
Two legs better!"
(Eight legs creepy!)

↑ GEORGE, is
THIS ABOUT SPIDERS?

ANIMAL FARM
by George Orwell
(1945)

Lord of the Flies

"as long as we have
the conch shell, we are —
wait, where is it?!"

Piggy had eaten it.
~~Piggy ate everything.~~

LORD OF THE FLIES
by William Golding
(1954)

In the future, the government will burn all of the books. All of the books except for "Fahrenheit 451" by Ray Bradbury. That book is the greatest book ever written, Better than that "1984" book by Orwell. That book is trash. REALLY RAY?

FAHRENHEIT 451
by Ray Bradbury
(1953)

"My name is Scout Finch.
What's yours?"

"Boo Radley."

"What's Boo short for?"

"Boobies."

TO KILL A MOCKINGBIRD
by Harper Lee
(1960)

An Occurrence at Owl Creek Bridge

A man stood at the edge of the bridge with a noose around his neck. He had been sentenced to death for being an owl.

"I'm not an owl!" he screamed.

"WE'LL SEE ABOUT THAT!" his captors yelled.

"Please, I'm a man," he pleaded, "don't kill me—"

Then he was hanged.

"AN OCCURRENCE AT OWL CREEK BRIDGE"
by Ambrose Bierce
(1890)

45

Atlas Hugged

"I need more steel for the railroads, Hank."

"Alright, but it's going to cost you 137,000 hugs."

"That sounds fair," said Dagny, "as long as there is an exchange of goods and services, and you're not a moocher."

Then they hugged 137,000 times.

ATLAS SHRUGGED
by Ayn Rand
(1957)

a Good Man Is Hard to Find

~~Was she single?~~

~~a Good Man Is Hard to Find~~
any man

a Disease ~~Free~~ Man

a Single Man

Not a jerk

~~Asshole~~

~~a non divorcé~~

JUST A Guy wHo iS
NOT AN ASSHOLE

"A GOOD MAN IS HARD TO FIND"
by Flannery O'Connor
(1953)

The Metamorphosis
by Franz Kafka

Gregor looked down at his body, now transformed into that of a giant insect. "Puberty!" he thought to himself "Finally!"

THE METAMORPHOSIS
by Franz Kafka
(1915)

"What have I got in my pocket?"
Bilbo wondered aloud.

"A dead fish," answered Gollum.

"What? No, that's disgusting. Guess again."

"Two dead fish."

"I already said no to one dead fish.
Why would it be two?
Guess again."

"Three dead fish."

THE HOBBIT
by J.R.R. Tolkien
(1937)

"The wargs are coming!" yelled
Gandalf, "Quick, into the trees!"

"What are wargs?" asked Bilbo

"Giant wolves!" Thorin aswered.

"Why cant we just call them
that?"

"It takes too long! wargs is
quicker."

"How often do you have to say "wargs"
that it's actually worth —"

Bilbo was eaten. The ~~giant wolves~~ wargs
had come.

THE HOBBIT
by J.R.R. Tolkien
(1937)

"But rings are for girls!" cried
Frodo, "and I'm not a girl, I'm
a hobbit!"

Gandalf stared at him silently,
then slowly raised his wizard
staff at him.

"Not for long!" Gandalf
yelled, zapping him with magic.

Sam watched from the window,
crying.

THE LORD OF THE RINGS: THE FELLOWSHIP OF THE RING
by J.R.R. Tolkien
(1954)

Out of nowhere a giant
spider called Shelob
emerged from the darkness.

"Oh HELL No!" Frodo screamed.

He took the ring off quickly,
threw it on the ground, and
ran.

"Keep it! I dont do Spiders!"

Sam stayed behind. And was
eaten.

THE LORD OF THE RINGS: THE TWO TOWERS
by J.R.R. Tolkien
(1954)

"Destroy the Ring!" Sam screamed at Frodo standing at the edge of Mount Doom.

"IT'S TOO PRETTY!" Frodo screamed back!

THE LORD OF THE RINGS: THE RETURN OF THE KING
by J.R.R. Tolkien
(1955)

"I'm Holden. What's your name?"
"My name is Phoney McPhoney Phoney"
Holden's head exploded.

THE CATCHER IN THE RYE
by J. D. Salinger
(1951)

"You're my best friend,
Pooh Bear."

"You're my best friend,
Piglet!"

"YOU ONLY EXIST IN
MY MIND" screamed
Christopher Robin from
his straight jacket

WINNIE-THE-POOH
by A.A. Milne
(1926)

The Giving Tree

Once there was a tree...
and she loved a little boy.

So she tried to adopt him,
and raise him as a tree boy.

But she didnt have hands, so
she couldnt hold the pen to sign
the adoption papers.

THE END.

SHEL, THIS IS FOR
CHILDREN??

THE GIVING TREE
by Shel Silverstein
(1964)

"~~Are you there, God?
It's me, Margar—~~"

"WHAT CAN I DO FOR
YA MARGARET?"

"Are you there, God?
It's me, Margaret."

No one replied. There was
silence. Because (God doesn't) ?
exist.

ARE YOU THERE GOD? IT'S ME, MARGARET.
by Judy Blume
(1970)

"I need to find an heir for the chocolate factory!" Willy Wonka said. "I have diabetes, and can't be around here anymore."

CHARLIE AND THE CHOCOLATE FACTORY
by Roald Dahl
(1964)

The Cat in the Hat

by ~~Dr.~~ Seuss NOT A REAL DOCTOR!

~~Mr. Seuss~~

Sr. Seuss

(Mrs. Seuss) ?

His Royal Seuss

Señor Seuss ← TOO SEXY

~~Seuss PhD~~

The Seuss

THE CAT IN THE HAT
by Dr. Seuss
(1957)

I do not like
green eggs and ham.
Also, I'm gluten free.

DOESN'T RHYME

GREEN EGGS AND HAM
by Dr. Seuss
(1960)

"We have to keep the garden
a secret."

"What garden?"

"Exactly."

THE SECRET GARDEN
by Frances Hodgson Burnett
(1911)

Deaf of a Salesman
By Arthur Miller

<u>Character List</u> (in order of appearance)

Willy Loman — a salesman (deaf)
Linda — his wife (deaf)
Biff — his son (deaf)
Happy — his son (deaf)
Bernard — neighbor's son (deaf)
The woman — Willy's mistress (deaf)

DEATH OF A SALESMAN
by Arthur Miller
(1949)

The Elephant Man

[Enter TREVES. He stares at MERRICK, confused.]

    Treves: Who are you?

    Merrick: The Elephant Man.

    Treves: Of course you are.

[Treves quickly hides his bag of peanuts.]

THE ELEPHANT MAN
by Bernard Pomerance
(1977)

Howl

I SAW THE BEST MINDS OF
MY GENERATION DESTROYED BY
MADNESS, STARVING HYSTERICAL NAKED
EXCEPT FOR WEARING TUBE SOCKS
SO NOT TOTALLY NAKED
BUT MOSTLY NAKED IF YOU
DON'T COUNT THE FEET.

"HOWL"
by Allen Ginsberg
(1955)

"Breakfast at Tiffany's"
by Truman Capote

|
who's got
time any more?

"a Quick Coffee at Tiffany's"

BREAKFAST AT TIFFANY'S
by Truman Capote
(1958)

Two roads diverged in a wood, and I—
I took the one less traveled by,
And I have been lost for forty five minutes

"THE ROAD NOT TAKEN"
by Robert Frost
(1920)

Waiting for Godot

by Samuel Beckett

Estragon: Let's go!

Vladimir: We can't

Estragon: Why not?

Vladimir: We're waiting for Godot.

[Godot pops out from behind the tree.]

Godot: Yoohoo! Did someone say Godot?

[They all embrace. Godot is the coolest. They walk off arm in arm.]

End.

WAITING FOR GODOT
by Samuel Beckett
(1949)

The Karlist Marxifesto

by Karl Marx

REALLY KARL?!

THE COMMUNIST MANIFESTO
by Karl Marx
(1848)

THUS SPAKE ZARATHUSTRA

Tod

~~God~~ is dead. Tod remains dead. And we have killed him. Yet his shadow still looms. The shadow of (Tod). How shall we confront ourselves, that now he is gone. WHO IS TOD?

65

THUS SPAKE ZARATHUSTRA
by Friedrich Nietzsche
(1883)

George: Who's afraid of —

Nick: Bees?!? I'm allergic. Deathly.

George: No, not bees. Virginia Woolf.

Nick: Is she a bee?

George: No. She's a —

Nick: Then no. Just bees.

WHO'S AFRAID OF VIRGINIA WOOLF?
by Edward Albee
(1962)

Konstantin walks into a Grocery store.

KONSTANTIN
  I would like a dozen red roses, a box of chocolates, and a card that says "I love you."

GROCER
  Fresh out. All we got left here is a couple of dead seagulls.

KONSTANTIN
  It's for a girl.

GROCER
  Girls love dead seagulls.

KONSTANTIN
  Fine. Give me one dead seagull-

GROCER
  We have a buy one get one half off deal-

KONSTANTIN
  Just one, thank you very much!

THE SEAGULL
by Anton Chekhov
(1895)

It is just Jim and Laura in the room now.

JIM

Can I have this dance?

He grabs Laura's hand and pulls her in close, but suddenly her hand snaps off.

JIM

What the-

He drops it, and it shatters on the ground. She is made of glass. So is the room. It is all glass. The world is glass. It all shatters.

Tom is angry.

THE END

THE GLASS MENAGERIE
by Tennessee Williams
(1944)

```
Stanley: Stella!

Stanley: STELLA!

Stanley:STELLLAAAAAAAAAAAAAAAAAAAAAAAAAA
AAAAAAAAAAAAAAAAAAAAAAAAAAAAAAAAAAAAAAAA
AAAAAAAAAAAAAAAAAAAAAAAAAAAAAAAAAAAAAAAA
AAAAAAAAAAAAAAAAAAAAAAAAAAAAAAAAAAAAAAAA
AAAAAAAAAAAAAAAAAAAAAAAAAAAAAAAAAAAAAAAA
AAAAAAAAAAAAAAAAAAAAAAAAAAAAAAAAAAAAAAAA
AAAAAAAAAAAAAAAAAAAAAAAAAAAAAAAAAAAAAAAA
AAAAAAAAAAAAAAAAAAAAAAAAAAAAAAAAAAAAAAAA
AAAAAAAAAAAAAAAAAAAAAAAAAAAAAAAAAAAAAAAA
AAAAAAAAAAAAAAAAAAAAAAAAAAAAAAAAAAAAAAAA
AAAAAAAAAAAAAAAAAAAAAAAAAAAAAAAAAAAAAAAA
AAAAAAAAAAAAAAAAAAAAAAAAAAAAAAAAAAAAAAAA
AAAAAAAAAAAAAAAAAAAAAAAAAAAAAAAAAAAAAAAA
AAAAAAAAAAAAAAAAAAAAAAAAAAAAAAAAAAAAAAAA
AAAAAAAAAAAA!!!!!!!!
```

A STREETCAR NAMED DESIRE
by Tennessee Williams
(1947)

"I will give you a knife and a three hour head start," General Zaroff said. "Then we will play the most dangerous game."

Rainsford nodded. "Scrabble it is then."

"THE MOST DANGEROUS GAME"
by Richard Connell
(1924)

Slaughterhouse-Five

"We are aliens", they said to
Billy. "Call us Tralfamadorians. "

"Italians!" Billy nodded vigorously.

SLAUGHTERHOUSE-FIVE
by Kurt Vonnegut
(1969)

We Real Cool

We real cool. We
lef school. We
are unemployed.

"WE REAL COOL"
by Gwendolyn Brooks
(1959)

CONTEM
LITERAT

"When you play a game
of thrones, you win or you
die," Cersei said as she
picked up the dice.
"It is similar to
Monopoly in that aspect."

How Do
You PLAY
MONOPOLY

Eddard nodded. Monopoly
was his least favorite game.

A SONG OF ICE AND FIRE: A GAME OF THRONES
by George R.R. Martin
(1996)

"I want a massive dragon across my back," Lisbeth said.

"Are you sure?" asked the tattoo artist. "These things are forever."

"You're right. I'll give it some more thought, Thanks." Lisbeth left the tattoo parlor.

STIEG, THE TITLE MAKES NO SENSE NOW....

THE GIRL WITH THE DRAGON TATTOO
by Stieg Larsson
(2005)

"Welcome to Jurrarrassiric Park!"
Hammond screamed.

"What's it called?" Dr. Grant yelled back.

"Jurrrarrassricric Park!" Hammond replied.

"Come again?"

"Jurrrrrrarrassrrrrrrcir Park!"

"What are you saying?"

"Jurrrrrrrrrrrarrrrr..."

Hammond was having a stroke

Then the raptors came.

JURASSIC PARK
by Michael Crichton
(1990)

"There's another island with more dinosaurs! Do you want to go?"

"Are you talking about Rhode Island?"

"Nope."

"Then No thank you!"

THE LOST WORLD
by Michael Crichton
(1995)

Sixty-Nine Shades of Grey

by E L James

Really?.

FIFTY SHADES OF GREY
by E L James
(2011)

"You're not black?!" Harry exclaimed.

"Nope, it's just my last name," said Sirius.

Harry began to cry. He had still never met a black person.

HARRY POTTER AND THE PRISONER OF AZKABAN
by J.K. Rowling
(1999)

The Goblet suddenly started sputtering
for a fourth time, then spat out another
slip of paper. Dumbledore grabbed
it and read it aloud.

"Harry Pooter."

"Albus," whispered McGonagall, "I
think you mean 'Potter'."

"No. I meant what I said. Pooter.
Harry Pooter."

"Just put your glasses on."

Dumbledore put them on, then
tried again.

"My mistake! Harry Pooooter."

Ron was jealous.

HARRY POTTER AND THE GOBLET OF FIRE
by J.K. Rowling
(2000)

"We will call ourselves the D. A." Harry explained, "which stands for —"

"Daryl's Apples!" Daryl shouted out.

"Perfect," said Harry.

Ron was jealous.

who is Daryl?

HARRY POTTER AND THE ORDER OF THE PHOENIX
by J.K. Rowling
(2003)

"You can speak Parseltongue?" asked Hermione.

"And Italian, Spanish, and French!" Harry replied. "Pretty much all the Romance languages."

Ron was jealous.

HARRY POTTER AND THE CHAMBER OF SECRETS
by J.K. Rowling
(1998)

"There were four Deathly Hallows,"
explained Hermione, "the Elder
Wand, the Invisibility Cloak, the
Resurrection stone, and the
Wacky Wig."

Jumbo shoes

Helicopter Hat   Clown?

Fat suit

Trampoline shoes

HARRY POTTER AND THE DEATHLY HALLOWS
by J.K. Rowling
(2007)

Glenngarry ~~Glen Ross~~

Glengarry (Glenrossy)

Glen ~~Glen~~ ~~Glen~~ Ross

~~Gaaaaaarry~~

~~Gleeeen~~

Mr. Garry

~~Glen and Gary~~

(Men Cursing and Yelling)

GLENGARRY GLEN ROSS
by David Mamet
(1983)

Marley and Me

by John Grogan

Cats can go to hell.

Nobody cares when a cat dies.

They're just awful.

we get it. you're a dog person.

MARLEY AND ME
by John Grogan
(2005)

"My name is Isabella,"
I said to him, "but
everyone calls me Bella."
He looked at me with
his beautiful deep eyes.

"Well I will call you
Isa."

TWILIGHT
by Stephanie Meyer
(2005)

83

THE DA VINCI CODE

"I KNOW WHO KILLED JACQUES!"
ROBERT SAID EXCITEDLY.

"WHO?"

"LEONARDO DA VINCI!" literally
impossible

THE DA VINCI CODE
by Dan Brown
(2003)

"You're a ~~wizard~~ plumber, ~~Harry~~ Jeffrey!" ~~Hagrid~~ Hagroid said.

"a ~~wizard~~ plumber?" asked ~~Harry~~ Jeffrey

JK, THIS ALL SOUNDS FAMILIAR.

THE CASUAL VACANCY
by J.K. Rowling
(2012)

~~Eat, Pray, Eat~~ TOO MUCH EATING
by Elizabeth Gilbert

Eat, Pray, ~~Sleep~~

Eat, Pray, Love

~~Eat, Pray, Read~~

Eat, Eat, Eat TOO MUCH EATING

Eat, (Prey), Love — HUNTING ??

EAT, PRAY, LOVE
by Elizabeth Gilbert
(2006)

The Kite Runner

" Hassan, you are the best kite runner in the city."

" Thank you, Amir."

" This year, I want you to be the kite."

" For you, a thousand times over."

Amir tied a long piece of string to Hassan's ankle, and began to run.

PHYSICALLY IMPOSSIBLE

THE KITE RUNNER
by Khaled Hosseini
(2003)

The boy from District 9
swings his sword, but
right before it hits me
a croissant flies out of
nowhere and hits him in
the eye.

"Peeta!" I scream

THE HUNGER GAMES
by Suzanne Collins
(2008)

FILM

TELEV

                    HARRY
         You don't think that I can tell the
         difference? Get outta here.

Sally looks around the restaurant for a moment, then
begins to fake an orgasm. She starts by moaning and
panting, then builds into a full screaming orgasm.

                    SALLY
         Oh. Ohhhh. Oh yes. OH YES. YES.
         YEEESSSSS. Oh BABY. YEEESSSSSS.

Everyone in the deli stares and Harry looks at his
food, embarrassed. An old woman next to them turns to
her waiter and orders.

                    OLD LADY   not a real thing
         I'll have the orgasm sandwich.

WHEN HARRY MET SALLY
directed by Rob Reiner
[screenplay by Nora Ephron]
(1989)

                    TOMMY (CONT.)
        You think I'm funny? What exactly
        is so funny? Do I look like a clown
        to you? Do I?

Sal nods. Tommy is wearing a red nose and giant shoes.

            ISN'T HE IN
            THE MAFIA?

GOODFELLAS
directed by Martin Scorsese
[screenplay by Nicholas Pileggi and Martin Scorsese]
(1990)

Starling sits on the opposite side of the glass
and pulls out a folder.

                    STARLING
          I see in your file that you're a
          vegetarian?

                    LECTER
          Nope. I'm the cannibal.

                    STARLING
          Which one is that again? Is that no
          animal by-products or like you can
          still eat fish?

                    LECTER
          I eat people.

                    STARLING
          Oh.... OHHHH. Now this whole
          'prison' thing makes sense haha.
          Ok. Moving on.

THE SILENCE OF THE LAMBS
directed by Jonathan Demme
[screenplay by Ted Tally]
(1991)

The Scottish warriors turn their backs
to the English and drop their kilts.
They moon them. Their butts are out and
they are smacking them and screaming
"Woooooo!" and just smacking their butts.
Big butts. Little butts. Pale butts. Butts
butts butts. The English get angry and
shoot arrows but the butts are still there.
Butts are everywhere. Butttts -> (_|_)

Mel,
Is this Necessary?

BRAVEHEART
directed by Mel Gibson
[screenplay by Randall Wallace]
(1995)

INT. ROCKY'S APARTMENT - EARLY MORNING

Rocky gets out of bed and walks to his fridge. He pulls out
a dozen eggs and cracks them into a glass

> ROCKY
> Mmmmm... Chicken blood!

— SLY, THIS IS NOT WHAT EGGS ARE.

He drinks the whole glass, then goes outside to start his
workout.

EXT. APARTMENT - MOMENT LATER

Rocky stretches quickly, then starts running.

> ROCKY
> That chicken blood is giving me so
> much energy! The energy of dead
> chickens. And their blood.

ROCKY
directed by John G. Avildsen
[screenplay by Sylvester Stallone]
(1976)

Chief Brody leans overboard, dumping chum into the water. Suddenly, the shark breaks the surface and Brody sees just how big it is. He stumbles back into Cabin.

> CHIEF BRODY
> You're gonna need a bigger boat.

submarine

lot of guns

giant nets

an equally large
but good shark ?

a robot shark

army of dolphins

a fishing pole that is
actually four shotguns

JAWS
directed by Steven Spielberg
[screenplay by Peter Benchley and Carl Gottlieb]
(1975)

                    WALT
          I got cancer, a wife who's
          pregnant, a son with cerebral
          palsy, and a shitty job. I need to
          start making money. I need to start
          cooking-

Walt pulls out a chefs hat.

                    WALT
          Spaghetti.

                    JESSE
          Oh you crazy Mr. White!

BREAKING BAD
created by Vince Gilligan
(2008)

Restaurant Name Ideas

The Chicken Brothers —Too plain

(Los Pollos Hermanos)

Las Pollas Hermanas ??

Too obvious →
Las Drogas Hermanos

~~Pollos y Metanfetamina~~ No!

Kentucky Fried Methamphetamine are you kidding?

NO! ~~Meth, Meth, Meth~~

This Is A Regular Chipotle
↳ we need to talk...

BREAKING BAD
created by Vince Gilligan
(2008)

LOST - Final Episode

Jack is on his back and bleeding. He is about to die and is fading out.

CAMERA ZOOM IN ON HIS LEFT EYE

His eyes shut.

AND THEN THEY OPEN!

What's this? Jack is still alive???

Guess we'll have to wait to see what happens on season 7!

No. Rewrite ASAP

LOST
created by J.J. Abrams, Jeffrey Lieber, and Damon Lindelof.
(2004)

Mad Men
Angry Guys
Mad Men
Ad Men
Mad Guys
The Marketeers
Women are Dumb
Smoking + Drinking
Nice Suits

MAD MEN
created by Matthew Weiner
(2007)

EXT. PARK - DAY

"Christmas Time Is Here" plays as the children
ice skate on the frozen pond. SNOOPY begins to
skate, and he is really good. He does all sorts
of spins and flips. Suddenly, the ice starts to
crack, and all the children fall into the
freezing water. They are screaming for help.

REWRITE

CHARLIE BROWN watches from the side.

                    CHARLIE BROWN

          I guess that's what Christmas is
          all about.

The End. TOO SHORT

100

A CHARLIE BROWN CHRISTMAS
directed by Bill Melendez
[written by Charles M. Schulz]
(1965)

EXT. CHURCH - MOMENTS LATER

Benjamin and Elaine run out of the church and
jump into a bus that is just pulling away. They
make their way to the back row and sit down,
sweaty and exhausted.

They sit staring forward for a moment, and then
glance at each other.

Then Benjamin starts to sing.

>BENJAMIN
>
>The wheels on the bus go round and
>round, round and round, round and
>round. The wheels on the bus go
>round and round, all day long.

Elaine stares at him.

>BENJAMIN
>
>The horn on the bus goes beep bee-

>ELAINE
>
>TURN THE BUS AROUND!

THE GRADUATE
Directed by Mike Nichols
[screenplay by Calder Willingham and Buck Henry]
(1967)

Johnny storms into the show to Frances' table.

>   JOHNNY
>
>   Nobody puts Baby in a corner.

He reaches behind Frances and pulls a BABY out
from the corner.

>   JOHNNY
>
>   Let's dance!

He dances with the baby. The baby is a great
dancer. They win.

DIRTY DANCING
Directed by Emile Ardolino
[screenplay by Eleanor Bergstein]
(1987)

The men all start playing volleyball. It's hot out, so
Maverick takes his shirt off. So does Iceman. Then Goose
takes his pants off.

                    MAVERICK
          Oh c'mon Goose!

                    GOOSE
          This is why they call me Goose!

They all have a laugh, and then keep playing volleyball for
3 hours and sweating lots.

FADE TO BLACK.

End.

what happened to the airplane stuff??. Re write!

TOP GUN
directed by Tony Scott
[screenplay by Jim Cash and Jack Epps Jr.]
(1986)

                    RICK
Of all the gin joints in all the
towns in all the cities in all the
states in all the countries in all
the worlds in all the universes in
all the known galaxies in all the
dimensions, and assuming the
regular notion of the space time
continuum, she walks into mine!

CASABLANCA
directed by Michael Curtiz
[screenplay by Julius J. Epstein,
Philip G. Epstein, and Howard Koch]
(1942)

Wesley sits and takes his boots off. He pours rocks out
of them, and gets ready to fight Inigo.

             INIGO MONTOYA
        I do not mean to pry, but you don't
        by any chance happen to have six
        fingers on your right hand?

Wesley lifts up his right hand. He has eight fingers
on it.
             WESLEY
        I wish.

THE PRINCESS BRIDE
directed by Rob Reiner
[screenplay by William Goldman]
(1987)

Wendy walks down to Jack's desk slowly. She is terrified he
might see her, and is quiet. She begins to go through his
manuscript. On each page the same line: "All work and no
play makes Jack a dull boy" is written over and over.
Hundreds of pages of just this. She starts getting
increasingly agitated and frightened, and screams when a
voice erupts from behind her.

                    JACK
          Do you like it?

                    WENDY
          I think it could use some plot
          development, and maybe some more
          well rounded characters.

                    JACK
          It's just a first draft...

THE SHINING
directed by Stanley Kubrick
[screenplay by Stanley Kubrick and Diane Johnson]
(1980)

Diane Keaton

By

Woody Allen

ANNIE HALL
directed by Woody Allen
[screenplay by Woody Allen and Marshall Brickman]
(1977)

OPENING: ~~125~~ 180 minutes of black and white shots of Manhattan.
Rhapsody in Blue by George Gershwin plays the entire time.
I know it's only 16½ minutes long--loop the goddamn thing.

                    WOODY ALLEN

          I love New York City.

                                              Woody. 2

Fade to black

Fin.

MANHATTAN
directed by Woody Allen
[screenplay by Woody Allen and Marshall Brickman]
(1979)

Mary, still soaking wet from the dance, throws a
rock at the old house and makes a wish.

> GEORGE
>
> What'd you wish Mary?

> MARY
>
> I can't tell you it might not come
> true!

> GEORGE
>
> Come on, what is it you want Mary?
> You want the moon? Just say the word
> and I'll throw a lasso around it and
> pull it down.

> MARY
>
> I'll take it!

George nods and looks up at the moon slightly confused.
He picks up a bit of rope from the ground and throws it
up towards the moon. He tries again and again. He jumps
up and throws it at the moon, with no luck. He looks
back at Mary with tears in his eyes.

> GEORGE
>
> It's too high.

> MARY
>
> Typical!

IT'S A WONDERFUL LIFE
directed by Frank Capra
[screenplay by Frances Goodrich, Albert Hackett,
Frank Capra, and Jo Swerling]
(1946)

Sal drops a dead fish on the table.

                    SONNY

     What the hell is this?

                    SAL

     It's a Sicilian message. It means
     that they turned Luca Brasi into a
     fish.

                    SONNY

     WHAT?

THE GODFATHER
Directed by Francis Ford Coppola
[screenplay by Mario Puzo and Francis Ford Coppola]
(1972)

                    MICHAEL

     My father taught me many things, and
     he taught me this rule. He taught me:
     keep your friends close, and your best
     friends super-duper close.

                    FRANK

     What a kind old man.

109

THE GODFATHER: PART II
directed by Francis Ford Coppola
[screenplay by Francis Ford Coppola and Mario Puzo]
(1974)

Sergeant Hartman walks down the line of privates, inspecting
their person and footlockers. He stops when he gets to
Private Pyle.

                    SGT. HARTMAN
          Why is your footlocker unlocked?

                    PVT. PYLE
          I don't know sir!

                    SGT. HARTMAN
          Well now! Let's just see if there's
          anything missing!

Sergeant Hartman dumps the footlocker out. Inside, he finds
a jelly doughnut.

                    SGT. HARTMAN
          Holy Jesus. What is that?! What is
          that Private Pyle??

                    PVT. PYLE
          Sir, it's a doughnut sir!

                    SGT. HARTMAN
          It looks like a bagel, shit head!

                    PVT. PYLE
          Sir, doughnuts are like dessert
          bagels, sir!

beat.

                    PVT. PYLE
          Have you never seen a doughnut
          before sir?

                    SGT. HARTMAN
          NO I HAVE NOT PRIVATE PYLE SO SHUT
          YOUR GODDAMN MOUTH.

110

FULL METAL JACKET
directed by Stanley Kubrick
[screenplay by Stanley Kubrick, Michael Herr, and Gustav Hasford]
(1987)

E.T.~~A.F.G.I.L.H.~~
The Extra-Terrestrial ~~Alien Friendly Guy I Love~~ Him

By

Melissa Mathison

E.T. THE EXTRA-TERRESTRIAL
directed by Steven Spielberg
[screenplay by Melissa Mathison]
(1982)

                    ROSE
        I'm flying Jack! I'm flying!

Wings sprout out of Rose's back and she flies away, leaving
Jack alone on the ship.

                    JACK
        Not again! I have the worst luck!

Then the ship hits an iceberg and Jack dies.

TITANIC
directed by James Cameron
[screenplay by James Cameron]
(1997)

                    NICE GUY EDDIE
        Wait someone didn't tip.

                    MR. PINK
        I don't tip.

                    MR. WHITE
        What? Why not?

                    MR. PINK
        There was a hair in my coffee.

                    MR. BLONDE
        WHAT?

Mr. Blonde pulls out a gun and shoots the waitress in the
head.

RESERVOIR DOGS
directed by Quentin Tarantino
[screenplay by Quentin Tarantino]
(1992)

CAPTAIN KOONS (CONT.)
This watch. This watch was your
daddy's wrist watch when he was
shot down over Hanoi. He was
captured, put in a Vietnamese
prison camp. The way your dad
looked at it, that watch was your
birthright. So he hid it in the one
place he knew he could hide
something. His ass. Five long
years, he wore this watch up his
ass. Then he died of dysentery, and
he gave me the watch. I hid this
uncomfortable hunk of metal up my
ass two years. Then, after seven
years I was sent home to my family.
And now little man, I give the
watch to you.

BUTCH
Don't want it.

CAPTAIN KOONS
What?

BUTCH
It's a butt watch. I don't want it.

Quentin, why?

Captains Koons looks defeated. He looks at the watch in his
hand.

CAPTAIN KOONS
Guess it's back in the butt for
you.

PULP FICTION
directed by Quentin Tarantino
[screenplay by Quentin Tarantino and Roger Avary]
(1994)

                        DJANGO
              Now I'm gonna kill each and every
              one of you.

Django pulls out a pistol and begins to shoot bad guys.

Bang bang BANG BANG BANG BULLETS GUNS BULLETS BANG blood
blood blood bloooood blood bloodBLLOODD ullets guns GUNS
blood BANNGBANGBANGANBAN Bang bullets bang bang bang guns
blood blood blood bloooood bludod BANGB BANG GUNS BLOOD bang
bang

                        WHITE GUY
              I'll kill you nig-

EXPLOSION.

Django makes his horse dance for 25 minutes.

                                        10 minutes
                                         1 minute

DJANGO UNCHAINED
directed by Quentin Tarantino
[screenplay by Quentin Tarantino]
(2012)

                    BILLY
          I'll take a cranberry juice.

A man sitting next to him at the bar snorts.

                    MAN
          My girlfriend drinks that when
          she's on her period. What are you,
          my girlfriend?

Billy pulls his wig off and reveals that he's actually
Sarah, the man's girlfriend. Then she smashes an ashtray on
his head.

THE DEPARTED
directed by Martin Scorsese
[screenplay by William Monahan]
(2006)

Argo

Directed by Ben Affleck

Characters:

Mr. Argo: Matt Damon

Mr. Argo's best friend: Ben Affleck

Mr. Argo's best friend's little brother: Casey Affleck

Mr. Argo's mentor/professor: Robin Williams

Setting:

Iran: Boston   CALL MATT

ARGO
directed by Ben Affleck
[screenplay by Chris Terrio]
(2012)

INT. HOUSE

Harry opens the door, setting off a mini flamethrower. This
burns through Harry's hat, hair, and skull. It burns through
his head and brain. He is dead.

Then Marv comes in, trips, on his body, and falls on a nail
which goes through his head. He is dead too. There is blood.

Kevin watches smiling. He begins to laugh.

            KEVIN
    HAHAHAHAHAhahahaHAHa hahahaa
    haHAHAh hahhahhhhaaaaa
    hahahahhahahaahahhhhaaaaaa hhhaa

This is terrifying.

HOME ALONE
directed by Chris Columbus
[screenplay by John Hughes]
(1990)

Sex and the City

City and the Sex

Sexy City

Havin' Sex ~~in~~ the City
~~with~~
~~in~~ and

Intercourse and the Metropolis

Bangin and the ~~██~~ Big apple

Sex + City = (Sexity)

SEX AND THE CITY
created by Darren Star
(1998)

DANNY
And we will call them Ocean's 11.

RUSTY
Like after the ocean?

DANNY
No. After me. Danny Ocean.

RUSTY
Why not Rusty's 11?

DANNY
That sounds like a bunch of rusty
old nails.

RUSTY
I'm going to quit.

DANNY
FINE. Rusty's 11. You win.

Can't call it that.

OCEAN'S ELEVEN
directed by Steven Soderbergh
[screenplay by Ted Griffin]
(2001)

EXT. SPACECRAFT WIRING - SAME

Oxygen flows and pipes burst, rocking the spacecraft and the
astronauts. Master alarms go off and start ringing.

INT. SPACECRAFT - SAME

              JACK
     We have a problem.

              JIM
     What did you do?

              JACK
     Nothing, I stirred the tanks.

INT. NASA CONTROL - SAME

              NASA CONTROL
     This is Houston, say again please?

              JIM
~~Houston, we have a problem.~~ →boring

Houston, we got an issue ∅

Houston, we got a bit of a bugaboo

Houston, we done and shit the bed

Houston, (something is beeping)

Houston, we ~~fucked~~ up

Houston, (Tod) dropped the ball again!

who is Tod?

APOLLO 13
directed by Ron Howard
[screenplay by William Broyles Jr. and Al Reinert]
(1995)

                    DOROTHY
        Shut up.

                    JERRY
        What?

                    DOROTHY
        You had me at 'hello.'

                    JERRY
        Really? That's all it took?

                    DOROTHY
        It's my favorite word.

                    JERRY
        Hello?

                    DOROTHY
        Yep.

                    JERRY
        So if I had said 'Hey'

                    DOROTHY
        Wouldn't have worked.

JERRY MAGUIRE
directed by Cameron Crowe
[screenplay by Cameron Crowe]
(1996)

                    TYLER
          There are a couple rules here at
          fight club. Listen up.

The crowd circles Tyler.

                    TYLER
          Rule number one: No girls at fight
          club.

                    ROBERT
          Ok!

                    TYLER
          Rule number two: No girls at fight
          club.

                    ROBERT
          Sounds good!   *Sexist?!*

                    TYLER
          Rule number three: No girls at
          fight club!

                    ROBERT
          Yep!

                    TYLER
          Rule number four: NO GIRLS AT FIGHT
          CLUB!

                    ROBERT
          Hear hear!

                    TYLER
          Rule number five: NOOOO GIRRLLSSS
          ATTT FIGHT CLUB

                    ROBERT
          Amen!

121

FIGHT CLUB
directed by David Fincher
[screenplay by Jim Uhls]
(1999)

                    ALFRED
Why do we fall, Master Bruce?

                    BRUCE
I tripped on my cape.

                    ALFRED
No, I mean metaphorically-

                    BRUCE
I tripped on my cape. What do you
mean?

                    ALFRED
It's a metaphor, meant to
illustrate my point.

                    BRUCE
The Metaphor? Is he in league with
Ra's al Ghul?

                    ALFRED
"He" is a literary device, sir.

why can't he
understand metaphors?

BATMAN BEGINS
directed by Christopher Nolan
[screenplay by Christopher Nolan and David S. Goyer]
(2005)

Harvey Dent, who is now badly burned, comes out from behind
a wall.

>   BATMAN
>   Harvey! I've been looking for you!

>   HARVEY
>   Call me Two Face.

>   BATMAN
>   Okaaayyyy...

Beat.

>   BATMAN
>   I think "Half-Face" makes more
>   sense.

>   JOKER
>   You know, I actually agree with
>   you.

>   HARVEY
>   FINE. Half-Face. Call me Half-Face.

THE DARK KNIGHT
directed by Christopher Nolan
[screenplay by Jonathan Nolan and Christopher Nolan]
(2008)

                    BATMAN
What's that thing on your mouth?

                    BANE
It's a mask.

                    BATMAN
It's only covering your mouth
though.

                    BANE
What's your point?

                    BATMAN
It's not hiding your face. It's a
terrible mask.

                    BANE
What are you? The mask police?

                    BATMAN
No, they're all in the sewers.

THE DARK KNIGHT RISES
directed by Christopher Nolan
[screenplay by Jonathan Nolan and Christopher Nolan]
(2012)

<u>Frien</u>ds   TOO BROAD

~~Hot Friends~~

2 (Hot Girls) and 4
Regular People

6 People IN New York   LONG
WHO all ~~Have Sex with~~
Each other over Time

(Joey's an Idiot)   PERFECT

~~Ross + Rachel = LOVE~~

FRIENDS
created by David Crane and Marta Kauffman
(1994)

Noah rows the boat back to the dock in the pouring rain.
Allie jumps off and begins to walk away, but stops and
turns suddenly.

> ALLIE
> Why didn't you write? Why? It
> wasn't over for me. I waited for
> you for seven years, and now it's
> too late.

> NOAH
> ~~I DON'T KNOW HOW TO WRITE.~~

Not cute ... illiterate?

THE NOTEBOOK
directed by Nick Cassavetes
[screenplay by Jeremy Leven]
(2004)

(500) DAYS OF HELL

INT. OFFICE - MORNING

Tom walks into his office building. Before he gets to his desk, he stops. There is a new girl in the office, and she is beautiful. He walks up to her.

     TOM
  Hi, my name is Tom.

He reaches out to shake her hand.

     HELL
  My name is Hell.

When they shake hands, she sucks his soul away. For 500 days.

     TOM
  Do you like the The Smiths??

change "Hell" to "Summer"

(500) DAYS OF SUMMER
directed by Marc Webb
[screenplay by Scott Neustadter and Michael H. Weber]
(2009)

A police officer pulls over Dom and walks up to his car window.

> OFFICER
> Do you know why I pulled you over?

> DOM
> I was going fast?

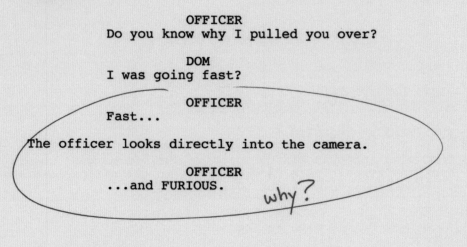

> OFFICER
> Fast...

The officer looks directly into the camera.

> OFFICER
> ...and FURIOUS.

why?

FAST & FURIOUS 6
directed by Justin Lin
[screenplay by Chris Morgan and Gary Scott Thompson]
(2013)

~~The Hurt Locker~~ ← *boring*

By

Mark Boal

The Boo Boo Room
The Ouchie Place

THE HURT LOCKER
directed by Kathryn Bigelow
[screenplay by Mark Boal]
(2008)

The King's S-s-s-s-s-s-p-p-peech

By

David Seidler

This is offensive

DAVID.

THE KING'S SPEECH
directed by Tom Hooper
[screenplay by David Seidler]
(2010)

                    DANIEL

          If you have a milkshake, and I have
          a milkshake, and I have a straw.
          And my straw reaches across the
          room, and starts to drink your
          milkshake. I drink your milkshake!

Eli leans in close.

                      ELI

          I'll just buy another milkshake.
          They're pretty cheap.

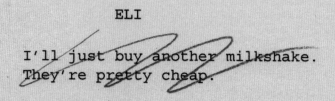

                      ELI

          When did we get milkshakes?

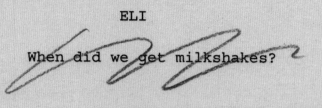

                      ELI

          Where did you get such a long
          straw?

THERE WILL BE BLOOD
directed by Paul Thomas Anderson
[screenplay by Paul Thomas Anderson]
(2007)

Lincoln ← Too easy

by Tony Kushner

~~Honest Abe~~

The Five Do~~lla~~ Bill Man

(A Penny for Your Thoughts:
the Abe Lincoln Story)

Honest ~~Babe~~

→ Too Tall for the Senate

Emancipator Proclimator

~~You Heard of the Cat?~~
~~Here's the President.~~

LINCOLN
directed by Steven Spielberg
[screenplay by Tony Kushner]
(2012)

                    BOBBY
          How many guns you got?

                    MARCUS
          Just one. How about you?

                    BOBBY
          One. Which means total we got...

They excitedly look at each other.

                    BOBBY AND MARCUS
               (simultaneously)
          Three guns!!

                    NOPE. MATH.

2 GUNS
directed by Baltasar Kormákur
[screenplay by Blake Masters]
(2013)

Clark Kent sits handcuffed behind a steel table.

> LOIS LANE
> You let them handcuff you?

> CLARK KENT
> Wouldn't be much of a surrender if
> I resisted... And if it makes them
> feel more secure, then...

Lois looks at the 'S' across his chest.

> LOIS LANE
> What's the 'S' stand for?

> CLARK KENT
> On my planet it stands for sexy.

> LOIS LANE
> We'll call you Sexyman.

NOT HIS — NAME

MAN OF STEEL
directed by Zack Snyder
[screenplay by David S. Goyer]
(2013)

too broad!

~~GIRLS~~ PILOT

by: Lena Dunham

(White) Girls

~~Girls~~ ?

~~Rich Girl Problems~~

Natural ~~Breasts~~

(Brooklyn!)

134

GIRLS
created by Lena Dunham
(2012)

                    SEAN PARKER
          Oh and guys, one last thing.

                        MARK
          What is it?

                    SEAN PARKER
          Drop the "facebook." Just "The."
          It's cleaner.

                        MARK
          "The.com" ... it's perfect.

Sean leaves.   didit happen

                      EDUARDO
          I hate him.

THE SOCIAL NETWORK
directed by David Fincher
[screenplay by Aaron Sorkin]
(2010)

ACKNOWLEDGMENTS

I'd like to thank Lino and Linda for raising me right and teaching me to love books; Anna, Anthony, Laura, and Giulia for the support only a *famiglia* can give; and Bianca, for everything.

Thanks to Kate McKean and the Howard Morhaim Literary Agency for reppin' me hard; Rachel Fershleiser and the wonderful people at Tumblr for the sweet lovin'; Steve Mockus and Chronicle Books for giving me a shot; Laura Ellen Scott and the English Department at GMU for the guidance; Dan Miller for the power of an introduction, and Cody James Clarke for a wonderful submission.

Also, thanks to the Good Sirs Sketch Group. You are all very good sirs.

ABOUT THE AUTHOR

Paul Laudiero is a writer and comedian who has studied with Washington Improv Theater and the Upright Citizens Brigade. His work has been featured on McSweeney's, CollegeHumor, Huffington Post, Mashable, and Wired. He lives in New York City.